My Visit To The Hospital

Sophie Davies
and
Diana Bentley
Reading Consultant
University of Reading

Photographs by
Trevor Hill

My Visit

My Visit to the Airport
My Visit to the Birthday Party
My Visit to the Dentist
My Visit to the Doctor
My Visit to the Hospital
My Visit to the Seaside
My Visit to the Supermarket
My Visit to the Swimming Pool
My Visit to the Zoo

First published in 1989 by
Wayland (Publishers) Limited
61 Western Road, Hove
East Sussex, BN3 1JD, England

British Library Cataloguing in Publication Data

Davies, Sophie
  My visit to the hospital.
  1. English language – Readers
  I. Title II. Hill, Trevor
  428.6

ISBN 1 85210 718 9

Typeset by L. George & R. Gibbs, Wayland
Printed and bound by Casterman S.A., Belgium

Contents

All words that appear in **bold** are explained in the glossary on page 22.

Hello, my name is Emma.

I am not feeling very well. I have a nasty cough. It makes my chest hurt.

My doctor said that I must have a chest **X-ray**. Mum has made an **appointment** at the hospital. She helps me to get ready to visit the hospital.

Dad takes me to the hospital.

My little brother Thomas comes too. Here we are arriving at the hospital.

Look at all these signs! We don't know which way to go. Where is the X-ray department?

Here is a **hospital porter**.

He works all over the hospital, so he knows the way. He tells us which way to go.

Here is the X-ray department. The
receptionist looks up my appointment. She
says we must wait a few minutes.

We wait in the waiting room.

There are lots of books in the waiting room.
Dad reads one to us.

This is the **radiographer**. Her name is Mrs Davies. She says it is time to have my X-ray. She gives me a special white **gown** to wear.

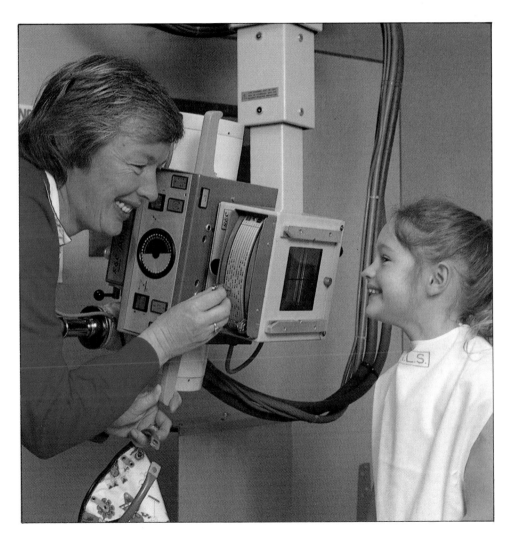

This is the X-ray machine.

Mrs Davies shows me the X-ray machine, and tells me how it works. It is like a special kind of camera.

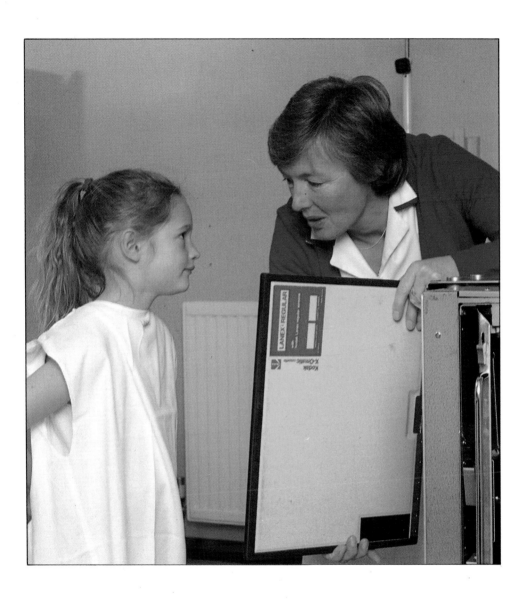

The X-ray machine has a film in it, like a camera. This is where the film goes.

Mrs Davies shows me how to stand.

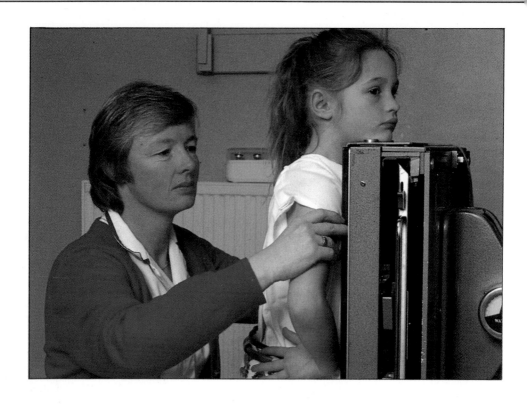

I put my hands on my hips and make sure my chest is close to the machine. I will have to breathe in for the X-ray. I try it first to practise.

Mrs Davies goes behind a special screen. She tells me what to do. I breathe in and hold my breath for a few seconds. The X-ray machine whirrs and clicks like a camera. It is taking a picture of my chest.

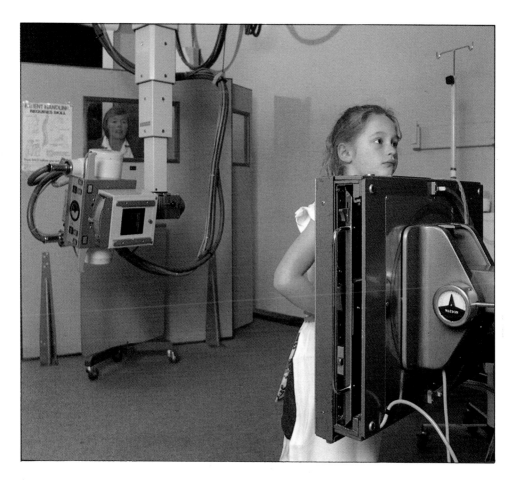

We wait for my X-ray photograph.

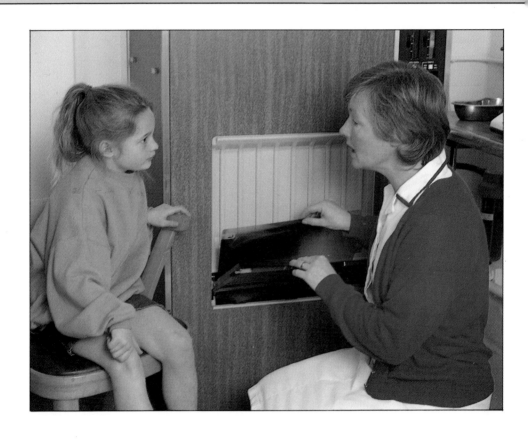

This machine develops the picture of my chest.
It takes less than two minutes.

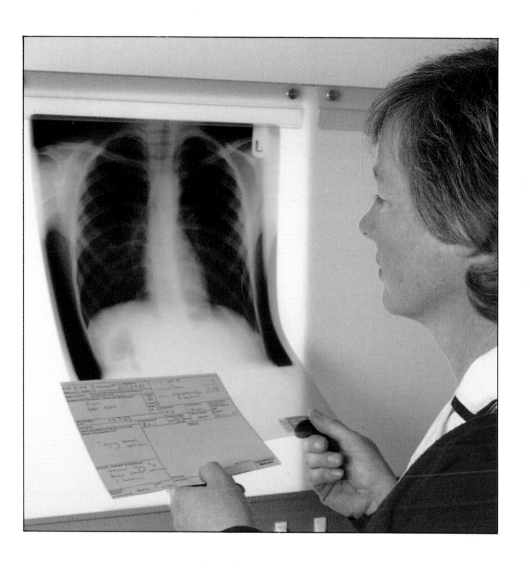

Now Mrs Davies looks at the picture of my chest. She sticks it to a box with a bright light. Now she can see clearly.

This is what my chest looks like inside.

Can you see my backbone and my ribs? Mrs Davies points to my lungs and my heart. Your chest looks like this too!

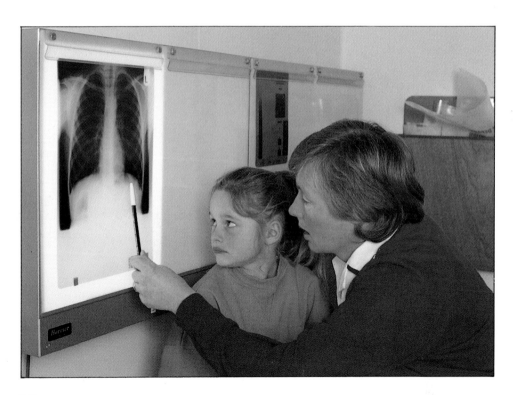

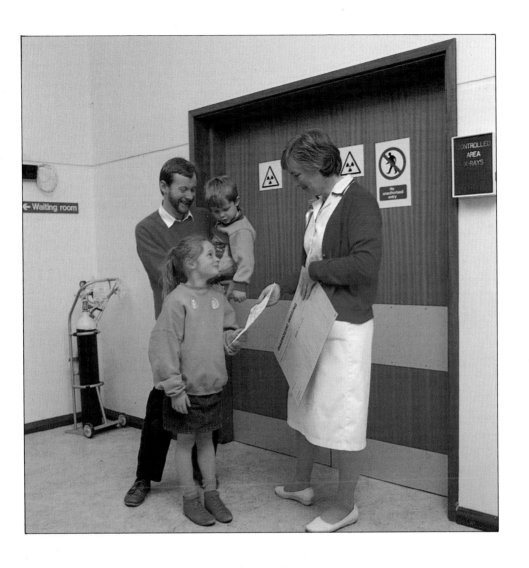

Now it is time to go. Mrs Davies gives me some badges and a special **certificate**. They say I am an X-ray film star!

Now I am better.

A few days later Mum rings the doctor. He says the X-ray showed that my chest is fine. Today my cough is much better.

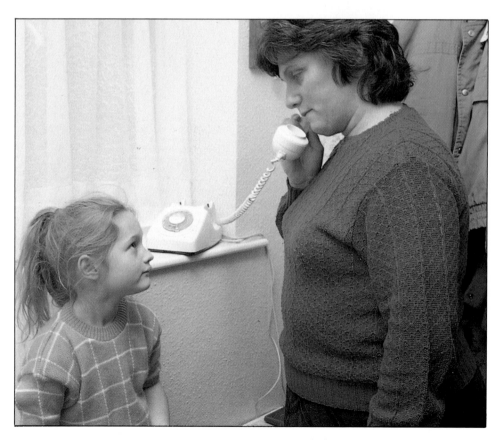

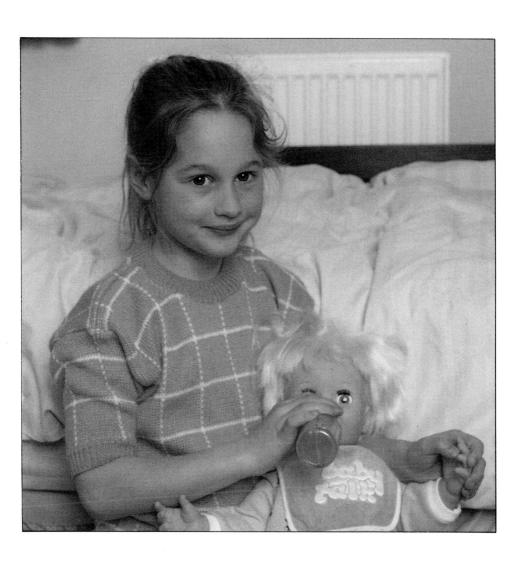

I enjoyed my visit to the hospital. I feel better now, and I am playing with my toys. Goodbye!

Glossary

Appointment The time that you arrange to see someone, like a doctor or dentist.

Certificate A piece of paper to show that you have done something, like swimming a length, or having an X-ray.

Gown A kind of dress that you wear in hospital.

Hospital porter A person who moves patients and trolleys with medicine and machines around a hospital.

Radiographer The person who takes X-ray photographs.

Receptionist The person who tells you when to come to the hospital.

X-ray A special photograph of the inside of your body. It helps the doctor to see if anything is wrong with you.

Books to read

Going to the Hospital Anne Civardi (Usborne, 1986)

Hospital John Colerne (Franklin Watts, 1987)

Linda Goes to Hospital Barrie Wade (A. & C. Black, 1981)

Why am I Going to Hospital? Claire Ciliotta (Angus & Ross, 1983)

Acknowledgements

The author and publishers would like to thank Emma Thompson, Thomas Rowlands, Janice Hill and the staff at the Queen Victoria Hospital, East Grinstead, Sussex, especially Richard Rowlands, Jean Davies, Tricia Thompson and Mike Smeed, for their help with this book.

Index